THE SPARE HEIR

BIOGRAPHY OF

PRINCE HARRY

Author

Bob's Premier Publishers Inc.

COPYRIGHT © BOB'S PREMIER PUBLISHERS INC. (2023)

All rights reserved. No part of this publication may be reproduced, distributed, or transmitted in any form or by any means, including photocopying, recording, or other electronic or mechanical methods, without the prior written permission of the publisher, except in the case of brief quotations embodied in critical reviews and certain other noncommercial uses permitted by copyright law.

INTRODUCTION

Prince Harry, 33 years old, stood nervously at the altar of St. George's Chapel in Windsor Castle, surrounded by friends, celebrities, and members of the royal family. The occasion was his wedding to Meghan Markle. Despite his familiarity with the castle, Harry felt out of place among guests who had arrived earlier in the day. The wedding was a grand event, with over 2,000 members of the public invited to the grounds, 600 high-profile guests inside, a security budget of over 2 million pounds, and millions of people watching live around the world. Harry fidgeted with his uniform, the formal dress of the Blues and Royals, as he thought about the new titles and responsibilities given to him by his grandmother, Queen Elizabeth II, that morning. He felt unprepared for the role of husband, a new function and title that carried less prestige but was life-changing nonetheless.

Today, Harry was getting married.

After what felt like an eternity, the bride finally arrived at the chapel. Meghan Markle, the American actress and blogger, wore a stunning white wedding dress designed by Clare Waight Keller of the French fashion house Givenchy. The dress featured a boat neckline, long sleeves and a sweeping train that was just slightly longer than the 16-foot silk veil. The entire dress was crafted from the finest silk and was a true work of art. Meghan made a strong statement of her feminist beliefs by walking down the aisle without a male escort, only accompanied by a group of junior attendants. She was greeted by the Prince of Wales who escorted her to the altar where Harry eagerly waited for her arrival. The love and adoration that shone on Harry's face, as captured by photographers and videographers, was a testament to the devotion he felt towards his wife. Though he was filled with love, Harry may have also experienced a touch of bittersweet emotions, wishing his mother, Princess Diana, could have been there to share in his special day. He may have also felt gratitude towards Meghan for helping him through a difficult time in his life, and a sense of pride in her for her strength and resilience in adapting to the world of a British Royal. Their love had brought them together, overcoming any obstacles that may have stood in their way.

First a Soldier, then a Prince

People in the United States and other parts of the world that are not members of the British Commonwealth do not know all that much about Harry, with the exception of the fact that he recently married Meghan Markle. The perceptive reader or viewer of news headlines is likely to recall that he was one of the two young men who lost their mothers as a result of the untimely passing of Princess Diana. The other young man was Prince Harry, who was also known as Harry Middleton. However, before he got married, he was involved in yet another significant aspect of his life that would occupy a significant portion of his adult life: the military. In point of fact, one could make the argument that Harry has been a soldier first and a prince second, and there are reasons for this that we'll go over later on in this book that we'll go over later on in this book.

We are going to discuss the ways in which Harry's early loss of his mother may have played a role in his decision to pursue a career in the military, as well as the ways in which this decision influenced a significant portion of the rest of his life. The fact that he was a member of the armed forces and fought on the front lines in Afghanistan did not determine everything else that took place in his life. On the other hand, as his career progressed, he shifted his focus to the servicemen and servicewomen who sacrificed their lives for their country while serving on the battlefield. It is considered "fortunate" that many of these people were able to survive the conflict despite having suffered severe wounds as a result of it. Those who were wounded severely enough that their lives were irrevocably changed as a result of their injuries, such as having a limb amputated, would bear the scars of war for the rest of their lives. As we will see in the following paragraph, Harry's experience motivated him to help people in a variety of different ways who suffered from such disabilities.

Understanding Prince Harry requires us to have a firm grasp on his past experiences as a member of the armed forces. On top of that, we need to look at the passing of his mother through the eyes of a young man who was already in a great deal of anguish due to the fact that his parents had divorced the previous year. This will help us understand how he felt about his mother's passing. We can't look at it through the lens of a conspiracy theorist who wants to blame Diana's death on anything from a conspiracy involving the royal family to evidence of an alien invasion. We can't do that. Instead, we need to consider the situation from the perspective of a young man who was already struggling to cope with the emotional fallout of his parents' separation.

In addition to analyzing Harry's life before he wed Meghan Markle, we will take a look at the occurrences that have completely redirected both of their lives in the wake of the widely publicized wedding day. The actual wedding day was shown all over the world via broadcast. Seeing Harry go from being a soldier to being a husband to now being an expatriate who lives in Southern California is a fascinating transition to watch unfold. As a result of this change, Harry and Meghan are now following a new and exciting path, albeit one that is also a little bit controversial.

This book takes an in-depth look at the life of Prince Harry from the perspectives mentioned above. We are going to go into a great deal of detail about Harry's childhood, including the difficulties that planted the seeds of trauma that would later grow into thorny vines to torment him. We are going to look into his academic and military preparation, as well as the challenges he had to overcome, in order to determine how he was able to participate in combat operations in one of the most dangerous places on the planet. And we'll see how he was pulled out of the abyss of hopelessness by reaching out to others and helping them, and then finally admitting to himself that he needed assistance as well. Both of these actions helped him pull himself out of the abyss.

In the end, we will see how Harry's experiences and the assistance he received helped him transform into a new version of himself, one who was prepared to take his relationship with an attractive and experienced young American woman to the next level. We will see how this post-transformation version of Prince Harry was willing to break away from the pressures and grandeur of royal life, turning his back on his roots in many different ways, in order to step into a new world and construct a new life for himself and his family.

This is the story of a young man who has been through an incredible amount of stress and tragedy, a young man who has allowed himself to be shaped by those experiences, and who has peered out into the abyss and been brought back from the brink of insanity. This is the story of a young guy who has been through an incredible amount of strain and tragedy.

This is the story of Henry Charles Albert David, more commonly referred to as Prince Harry around the world, and how he came to be in the form that he is in today.

CHAPTER 1

Heritage and Early Life

Prince Harry, who is a member of the Royal Family of the United Kingdom, has the opportunity to investigate his family tree and learn about his ancestry, which can be traced back many generations. When it comes to the question of when one could begin counting the royal lineage of the British Royal Family as opposed to the royal lineage of the rest of Europe, historians have a variety of opinions. However, King George III may be a good place to begin counting the lineage of the British Royal Family because, unlike his two predecessors (the first two Georges), George III was born in Great Britain (as opposed to Hanover, Germany, where his family was from), he spoke English as his mother tongue, and he lived in Britain for the entirety of his life. In addition, King George III was the first George to be crowned king of Great Britain. In 1801, the two kingdoms merged to form the United Kingdom, a new nation that George III ruled over for nearly 20 years until his death in 1820. George III's reign lasted until the United Kingdom's formation in 1801. Prior to the occurrence of this event, George III had served as King over both Britain and Ireland during their previous existence as two distinct states. This continued until George III's death in 1801, when it finally came to an end. It is generally accepted that King George III held the record for the greatest life span of any British monarch in the annals of British history, as well as the record for the longest reign of any British monarch.

George III's granddaughter was Queen Victoria, who was affectionately referred to as the "grandmother of Europe." She would go on to become the monarch of Great Britain for more than 63 years, making her the longest-reigning monarch over Britain up to that time (monarch, as opposed to King, because Victoria was a woman), surpassing King George III's 59-year reign and ushering in the Victorian Era. She would go on to become the longest-reigning monarch over Britain up to that time. Victoria was dubbed the "grandmother of Europe" during her reign. (Of course, Queen Elizabeth II, Harry's grandmother, will surpass Victoria's record by reigning for longer than 71 years until her death in 2022, at which point she will have surpassed the benchmark that Victoria set.)

The four children that were born to Elizabeth II and Philip, Duke of Edinburgh were named Charles, Anne, Andrew, and Edward. They were the offspring of the king and queen. Charles, who was born in 1948, would become Prince of Wales when he was ten years old and would eventually become King of the United Kingdom following Elizabeth's death in 2022. Charles would become King of the United Kingdom after Elizabeth's death in 2022. Charles II, who would now be known as King Charles II, ascended to the throne at the age of 73, making him the oldest person in the history of the British monarchy to ever be crowned King. He became known as King Charles II after his ascension to the throne.

Lord Mountbatten gave his advice to Prince Charles, telling him to choose a wife who was a good match for him in all aspects, such as having a pleasant personality and being physically attractive. It would turn out that Diana Spencer was the kind of girl who would be perfect for Charles in this role. On the other hand, they did not immediately begin a romantic relationship with one another right away. In point of fact, Diana was Charles's ex-younger girlfriend's sister. They dated when they were both much younger. Camilla was the name of the woman who was her older sister.

Harry's Mother And Father

The first time Prince Charles met Lady Diana was in 1977, when he was on his way to see Lady Diana's older sister. At the time, he was traveling with Lady Diana. However, at that time, he did not even consider the possibility that she could be his romantic partner. He did not even consider the possibility. Many people had the assumption that he would eventually get married to his cousin, a young woman whose name is Amanda

Knatchbull. In point of fact, this was the general consensus. Amanda was the granddaughter of Lord Mountbatten, the uncle of Prince Charles who had advised his nephew to "sow his wild oats far and wide" prior to getting married. Lord Mountbatten had been Amanda's great-grandfather. Amanda's great-great-grandfather was a man by the name of Lord Mountbatten. Despite the fact that Amanda was only 16 years old at the time, both of her parents agreed that she and Charles should get married as soon as it was socially acceptable for them to do so.

In the year 1980, Lord Mountbatten exerted a great deal of effort in an attempt to persuade Charles and Amanda to accompany him on a tour of India; however, he was ultimately unsuccessful in his efforts. In the end, the Irish Republican Army (IRA) was determined to be the organization responsible for the murder of Lord Mountbatten in 1979. Amanda was asked to become a member of the royal family by Prince Charles in 1980, but after the death of her grandfather, the young woman was hesitant to accept the proposal. Amanda's grandfather had been a member of the royal family. The relationship between the two parties ended not too much longer after that.

During the summer of 1980, Prince Charles made his first public display of interest in Diana, who continued to be a close friend throughout all of this time. When they first started spending time together, it was in a romantic capacity. On this particular occasion, Diana could tell that Charles was experiencing a low mood, so she made a concerted effort to cheer him up by using any and all means at her disposal. That was the point in time when, in the words of Charles' biographer, "without any obvious surge in feeling, he began to think seriously of her as a future bride," and he did so at that time. Additionally, that was the point in time when he did so. Almost immediately after that, they started dating, and Diana started accompanying Charles on his many excursions and engagements. Charles was the future king of the United Kingdom. Because of the media's preexisting interest in Princess Diana and the courtship, Prince Charles felt a great deal of pressure to make a decision regarding his future relationship with Diana. Because of this, Charles made the decision to make his proposal to Diana in February of 1981, despite the fact that those closest to him cautioned him that they didn't believe he was truly in love with Diana. Charles made this decision because he believed that Diana was the only person in the world who could make him happy. They had their hearts set on getting married in July of that very same year.

Diana was considered to be a celebrity both by the common people of the United Kingdom and by the media there. This is in part due to the fact that despite the fact that she was born into the British aristocracy, she possessed a quality that made her approachable and worldly, which enabled her to connect with the common people of the country and the world. Another reason for this is that despite the fact that she was born into the British aristocracy, she was able to connect with the common people of the world. She was brought up in a wealthy family and had a personal governess educate her at home for the first part of her education. She went on to achieve a high level of success in her chosen field. In spite of the fact that she never achieved a great deal of success in her academic endeavors, she continued her education at private schools and boarding schools in later years. After that, she spent the next few years bouncing around from job to job, during which time she occasionally gave lessons to students in music or dance and also worked as a nanny. She had ambitions in the past of becoming a teacher, despite the fact that her academic performance in school did not actually make that a viable option for her. Despite this, she had aspirations in the past of becoming a teacher. At that time, Prince Charles made his move and proposed to his girlfriend, Lady Diana Spencer. Diana was overcome with emotion at the prospect of joining the royal family, but she felt that she couldn't refuse the offer because she would be betraying the family's trust.

Diana and Charles moved into Kensington Palace not long after their wedding, which took place not long after Diana became the Princess of Wales at the age of twenty and married Prince Charles at the age of twenty. They also maintained a residence at Highgrove House, which is situated in the Tetbury neighborhood of Gloucestershire. By the time 1981 came to a close, Diana was already expecting her first child. Diana was experiencing symptoms of postpartum depression at the time of Prince William's birth in 1982. The year was 1982. The older brother of Harry is named William. After a period of time had passed, Diana discovered that she was expecting a child for a second time.

Her second son was born on September 15th, 1984, making him her second child overall. Henry Charles Albert David was christened in St. George's Chapel in Windsor Castle, the same place that would host his wedding many years later. The ceremony took place when Henry was just a baby. Everyone in the family, both in private and in public, referred to Henry Charles as "Prince Harry." Henry Charles was also known as "Prince Harry." This held true not only within the family but also beyond its confines. The monicker was kept, and to this day, it is the name that is most commonly used to refer to him.

Diana suffered from postpartum depression following the birth of her second son, William, but she eventually overcame this condition and was able to play an active and involved role in the upbringing of both of her sons. She was resolved to provide Harry and his older brother with a wide range of experiences, as opposed to just growing up in a castle, oblivious to the outside world, and as a consequence, she took Harry on a wide range of journeys. She also made sure that his older brother had a wide range of experiences as well. In many of these adventures, Harry's older brother, who was also a participant, joined him. For instance, in order to satiate their hunger, they would frequently visit McDonald's, just like any other young child in the UK would do. They followed in everyone else's footsteps and went to Disney World. However, Diana also made sure that the youngster was shown the more depressing aspects of the world by taking him to visit places like AIDS clinics and shelters for the homeless. In this way, she ensured that the youngster was adequately prepared for adulthood.

In addition, when Harry was still a young boy, he and his parents embarked on a number of adventures that took them all over the world. He embarked on his journeys of exploration at a young age and has since visited countries all over the globe, including Canada and Italy. Diana put a lot of effort into ensuring that Harry had a happy upbringing, but she was aware that once Harry turned 10, things were going to become a lot more challenging. Despite all of Diana's efforts, Harry's adolescence was not without its challenges.

National Tragedy

Up until the year 1987, Harry's parents were able to successfully conceal from the general public the majority of the difficulties that they experienced in their marriage. However, cracks began to appear in the relationship, particularly after the tabloids became involved in the controversy surrounding the matter. Since 1991, the couple had been living in separate locations, and by the time 1996 rolled around, they had already divorced and ended their marriage for good.

As a child, Harry had to go through some of the most difficult times of his life while he watched his parents ignore one another for extended periods of time, with the exception of their public appearances. These were some of the darkest years of Harry's life. It appeared as though they would never be together again, and in the end, that is precisely what happened: they never were together again after their breakup. Diana's struggles with postpartum depression and bulimia were well known, and she made no attempt to hide the fact that she struggled with these conditions. She did not make any attempt to conceal the fact that she was experiencing difficulties in her marriage either. The fact that Harry was made aware of these things will undoubtedly present him with difficulties in the years to come.

Then, on August 31, 1997, Diana passed away as a result of a car accident that occurred in Paris while she was moving at a rapid speed. Princess Diana's passing was lamented all over the world, and her funeral was one of the events in the annals of UK television history that attracted the highest number of viewers. When Harry and William were in Scotland, they stayed at the imposing Balmoral Castle, which is situated on an estate. Charles broke the news to his sons about Diana's passing, a bombshell that would continue to destabilize Harry's life for many years to come. Harry was only 12 years old when the news was delivered. During the funeral, Harry and his brother joined the rest of the Royal Family in walking behind Diana's carriage. They did this together with the rest of the Royal Family. They accomplished this feat in concert with the other members of the Royal Family.

Harry will never be able to move on with his life and will never be able to find closure as long as there is speculation about who might have been responsible for Diana's murder or whether it was, in fact, an accident. These theories will continue to torment him in the years to come and prevent him from ever finding closure. It was inevitable that he would have to mature quickly; however, as we will see in the chapters that are to come, he will finally discover a new purpose in life, something that will be able to rescue him from the turmoil that he is currently experiencing. On the other hand, before that could happen, he would have to put up with some difficulty as a student, as we will see in the chapter that comes after this one in the book.

CHAPTER 2

School Years

Following his early childhood education at Jane Mynors' nursery school in London, Prince Harry went on to complete his primary and secondary schooling at Wetherby School in Notting Hill, also located in the city of London. A number of famous people, such as the actor Hugh Grant, were educated at the illustrious Wetherby School, which is located in the city of London. This school is known for its high level of academic excellence. Because Prince Harry is a member of the British royal family, it is reasonable to suppose that he received his education at one of the country's prestigious private schools. After finishing his studies at Wetherby, Harry decided to continue his education at the Ludgrove School in Berkshire. In comparison to other independent schools in the United Kingdom, Ludgrove is regarded as a relatively progressive institution because its disciplinary expectations are less strict than those of other independent schools. Interactions take place between everyone, including the headmaster, teachers, and students; it is strongly encouraged that they become friendly with one another as a result of these interactions. Additionally, in order to hasten the process of maturation that takes place in the students, they are strongly encouraged to behave with a smidgen more autonomy. Classes at Ludgrove are typically small, with an average enrollment of no more than 12 students in most cases. This allows for a more personalized learning environment. Despite the fact that the school has a long tradition of sending boys to Eton, which is ultimately where Harry went to school, it has a reputation that is well-deserved for being a feeder for some of the best public schools and institutions in the United Kingdom.

Studying At Eton

Even though Harry had never known his mother, the paparazzi did their best to give him some privacy as he got older. Despite the fact that Harry had never met his mother. This is because the media and the British nobility have reached what is being referred to as a "pressure cooker agreement," which has resulted in this situation. This "invisible compact" stipulates that the media won't hound young members of the Royal Family, which enables them to concentrate on their studies and spend time with their friends instead of being harassed by the media. In addition, this "invisible compact" states that the media won't hound young members of the Royal Family. In return, all members of the Royal Family, regardless of their ages, have agreed to make themselves available for photographs and interviews at the times and places that have been previously arranged. As a consequence of this, once Harry had successfully completed his entrance examinations and had begun his studies at Eton, he was able to do so without any interference from members of the media. This was the case because Harry had already established his reputation as an exceptional student.

When it was decided that William and Harry would attend Eton, the decision was met with some opposition because it was a choice that not everyone agreed with. It has been a long-standing custom in the Mountbatten-Windsor family to send their children to Gordonstoun, a prestigious private school in Scotland that welcomes students of both sexes. Gordonstoun is located in the country of Scotland. It was here that Harry's great-grandfather, father, and two of his uncles were all laid to rest after they had passed away. On the other hand, Eton was the prestigious school that members of the Spencer family had attended for many generations. For instance, both Diana's father and brother obtained their educations from this particular establishment. As a consequence of this, Diana's recollections continued to have a sizeable and profound effect on the young men even after she had passed away.

One of the many fascinating ways in which Eton College stands apart from Gordonstoun is due to the fact that Gordonstoun is not one of Eton College's rival schools. To begin, it is a public school that can be found in the nation of England and its location. Second, this particular residential school does not accept any female students at any time. Eton has a long history of educating notable students, some of whom have gone on to hold powerful positions around the world or win the Nobel Prize. Eton also has a long history of educating students who have gone on to win the Nobel Prize. As a result of the high regard in which it is held across the Western world, Eton College has attained the status of a cultural icon in that region.

In the year 2001, when Harry was still a student at Eton, he broke his thumb while playing football for the school. Unfortunately, he needed a quick procedure on his thumb shortly thereafter; despite the fact that he required the procedure, he made a speedy recovery from it.

Harry successfully completed his coursework at Eton College and received two A-levels upon graduation in June of 2003.

When Harry was finally done with school, he came to the conclusion that it would be a wise decision to take a year off before continuing his education in some other capacity. Which particular field of labor did he wish to enter? Did he ever daydream about working in the medical field or in academia? Perhaps a position in the world of politics? No, he was set on doing one thing and one thing only, and that was joining the military, which is something that we will talk about in the following chapter. He had his mind made up about this.

Gap Year

Following his graduation from high school, Harry made the decision to make the most of his gap year by participating in some exciting activities. Despite the fact that Princess Diana has passed away, her legacy is still very much present in this area, as can be seen once again. It was not outside the realm of possibility that Harry would use the money provided by the Royal Family to travel the world in opulent fashion. He was able to socialize with some of the wealthiest and most powerful people in the world, as well as enjoy stays at luxurious resorts, thanks to the opportunities that were presented to him. Instead, he persisted in the line of reasoning that had led him and his brother to seek treatment at AIDS clinics and shelters for the destitute. Specifically, he persisted in the line of reasoning that had led him to seek treatment at an AIDS clinic. He moved to Australia with the goal of finding work as a jackaroo on one of the country's cattle stations once he got there. Harry worked with his hands in extremely hot conditions for several months while rubbing shoulders with the Australian equivalent of cowboys. The conditions were extremely hot. After that, he traveled to the tiny kingdom of Lesotho, which is situated in South Africa but is entirely encircled by that nation. Lesotho is a completely landlocked nation. While he was there, he contributed to the making of a documentary called The Forgotten Kingdom while also assisting in the development of orphaned children.

After finishing his gap year in 2004, he was ready to focus his concentration on the career path of his choosing. However, in order to do so, he needed to continue his education by enrolling in military training first.

CHAPTER 3

Military Training

Even before Harry took a year off to work as a cowboy in Australia, he had already begun preparing for a future in the military by enrolling in the Combine Cadet Force while he was still a student at Eton. This allowed Harry to get a head start on his future career in the military. The Combined Cadet Force, or CCF for short, is a military training program for students that is sponsored by the United Kingdom's Ministry of Defense. It is comparable to the Reserve Officers' Training Corps (ROTC) and Junior ROTC programs that are offered in the United States. The CCF was established in 1948 and has since grown to over 20,000 members. The British Community Cadet Force (BCCF) is a youth organization with the following mission statement: "to provide a disciplined organization in a school so that pupils may develop powers of leadership by means of training to promote the qualities of responsibility, self-reliance, resourcefulness, endurance, and perseverance." This mission statement can be found on the organization's website. The British Columbia Cadet Force (BCCF) is comprised of, among other things, branches representing the army, the royal navy, and the royal air force. A young member of the royal family who possessed such qualities would unquestionably find themselves in a position of advantage, even if they had no intention of serving in the armed forces as such. This is because of the prestige that comes with being a member of the royal family.

When Harry was in his final year at Eton, he had already been promoted to the rank of cadet officer, and he was in charge of leading the yearly march for the CCF at the Eton tattoo. Harry had been at Eton for four years. When Harry returned from his year off, he was ready to finish his official training at Sandhurst, where he had been previously stationed.

Royal Military Academy

If you want to work your way up through the ranks and become an officer in the British armed forces, you are going to have to enroll in one of these three schools. If you want to become a commissioned officer in either the Navy or the Air Force, your only options are to attend either Britannia Royal Naval College, which is located on a hill overlooking the port of Dartmouth in Devon, England, or Royal Air Force College Cranwell, which is part of the Royal Air Force base in Cranwell and boasts of being the world's first air Academy, having been founded in 1919. If you want to become a commissioned officer in either the Navy or the Air

Force, you must imagine that, much like Prince Harry, one of your ambitions is to have a successful career in the British Army. How would you go about accomplishing this goal? In that case, in order to finish your initial officer training, you will be expected to report to the Royal Military Academy Sandhurst, which is more commonly referred to simply as Sandhurst.

The fact that a member of the royal family, and a member of the combined cadet force at that, is not automatically granted acceptance into The Academy is a testament to the high standards that the school maintains in its admissions process. The grades that Harry received when he graduated from Eton played a significant role in his acceptance to Sandhurst, and the fact that he was accepted to Sandhurst played a significant role in Harry's grades during his time at Eton.

The teachers are held to the same rigorous expectations as the students in their classes. Noncommissioned officers from every branch of the British Army submit applications every year in the hope of being selected for one of sixty open positions, which are fiercely contested. After that, those individuals who are interested in becoming instructors will have to compete against one another in a challenging series of mental and physical tests; in the end, only thirty of them will be selected. This selection process, which can last anywhere from three to four weeks, is intended to ensure that the level of training that is provided is of the highest possible caliber possible. There is no other company or institution that makes potential instructors go through such a rigorous hiring process in order for them to become a part of the training team. This is something that is unique to our company. Contrary to what most people think, the age-old proverb that "those who can't do, teach" does not apply to the Royal Military Academy at Sandhurst. This is a common misconception.

When Harry first began his training at Sandhurst, it was in the month of May 2005. During the time that he spent there as a student, he was not addressed in the traditional manner that is customary for any member of the British royal family, which is to say, "your Royal Highness." Even less frequently than that, people would refer to him as Prince Harry. People generally referred to him by the title Officer Cadet Wales instead of that.

Roughly two hundred new cadets join the institution all at once each time it opens its doors. They are each assigned a spot in a platoon that falls under one of two companies; there are approximately one hundred cadets in each company. The Academy has the capacity to train up to ten distinct companies at the same time, and each company has its own unique name that is derived from a significant conflict or operation in the history of the British Army.

For example, Harry was assigned to the Alamein Company, which got its name from the town of El Alamein, which is located in Egypt and was the site of two battles during World War Two. Harry served in this company during the war. The "second battle of El Alamein" took place at the end of October and the beginning of November in the year 1942. This conflict is also referred to by its full name, the "Battle of El Alamein." It was an intense series of desert conflicts that resulted in a British victory that eliminated the Axis threat in Egypt and sparked the beginning of the end of the western desert campaign. The conflicts were between the British Eighth Army and Axis forces. The conflict took place in the sand dunes of Egypt's desert.

Officer Cadet Wales had successfully completed his officer training by the time April 2006 rolled around. At that time, he was presented with his commission as a Cornet, which is an obsolete term for a second Lieutenant. Officer Cadet Wales had completed his officer training by the time April 2006 rolled around. He was given a position in the Household Calvary, which is a subunit of the Household Division that helps to protect the King in a variety of official capacities. In this capacity, the King's safety is a primary concern. The Household Cavalry is responsible for a great deal more than just ensuring the safety of the royal family, despite the fact that this duty may not sound particularly interesting. Given that the Calvary is further subdivided into the two most senior regiments of the British Army, Harry's assignment to the Blues and Royals, also known as the Royal Horse Guards and 1st dragoons, was a tremendous honor for him. This is because the Blues and Royals are both part of the Calvary.

This task required a lot of movement and put the participant in a potentially dangerous situation. The Blues and Royals have been sent on missions to various locations around the world, including Northern Ireland, Germany, and Cyprus. They took part in the wars that broke out in the Falkland Islands in 1982, in Bosnia in the middle of the 1990s, and, most recently, in Iraq and Afghanistan. These conflicts all took place in the United Kingdom. In point of fact, back in 2006, it was announced that Harry's unit would be deployed to Iraq at some point during the course of the following year. This happened to be the case. Widespread outrage and controversy were sparked when it was questioned whether or not a prince should be allowed to take part in combat on the front lines. In the following chapter, we will discuss the challenges that need to be addressed, as well as how they influenced Harry's future as a commissioned officer and how they impacted the situation. In addition, we will discuss how these challenges impacted Harry's future.

Chelsy Davy

On the occasion of Harry's 21st birthday, he granted an interview to The Guardian, which is a prominent newspaper based in London and a leading online news source. Harry discussed his plans for the future. Despite the fact that the article covered a wide range of topics, including his father's relationship with Camilla Shand, among other things, the topic of Harry's romantic life was brought up and discussed. At this point in time, he had already started a relationship with Chelsy Davey, and it was one that was fraught with tension and involved interactions that were both intermittent and continuous. During the course of the interview, Harry made the following remarks regarding his girlfriend: "I wish I could tell everyone how incredible she is, but the moment I start talking about that, I am exposing myself to the possibility of criticism. I really wish I could tell everyone how incredible she is. There are lies, and I regret to say that I am unable to share the truth with you. There is a distinction that can be made between the two." The next chapter will touch on the fact that the general public had a difficult time discovering the facts about the nature of the relationship that existed between Harry and Chelsy, which will be covered in more detail in the following chapter.

Chelsy Davy, Harry's younger sister by one year, is named after Chelsy's father, Zimbabwean businessman Charles Davy, a safari farmer who was once one of the wealthiest landowners in Zimbabwe. Charles Davy was once one of the wealthiest landowners in Zimbabwe. Chelsy Davy, who is Charles Davy's daughter, is Harry's younger sister by one year. Chelsy was sent to a boarding school in England, and it was during her time there that she was introduced to Harry for the very first time. When Chelsy had the interview with Harry that was described earlier in 2005, she was in the midst of completing her undergraduate degree in economics at the University of Cape Town, which is located in the country of South Africa. On the other hand, she was successful in completing her undergraduate degree in 2006, after which she relocated to England and enrolled in the law program at the University of Leeds.

Chelsy would continue to play a significant role in Harry's life for a good number of years to come after they first met. But we'll go into more detail about that in a little while.

CHAPTER 4

Afghanistan and Back

In days gone by, a specific kind of prince would join his men on the frontlines of combat. This would serve several purposes: it would boost the morale of his troops, it would allow him to coordinate the battle strategy in real time, and it would set an example of strength and bravery for his troops to follow. Because the King was aware that his value on the battlefield was determined by a variety of factors other than how well he could swing a sword or act, it was only natural for him to avoid engaging in reckless behavior. Instead, he would encircle himself with his most powerful warriors as a means of self-defense as well as a demonstration of the power of the royal family. This was done in order to show off the strength of the royal family. On the other hand, there is no record of any ancient or medieval ruler ever having to be concerned about the possibility that a single Hellfire missile or strategically placed mortar could end his life and the lives of everyone in his immediate vicinity.

As soon as it was made known to the general public that Prince Harry's unit would be serving in Iraq the following year, a heated discussion about whether or not a member of the royal family ought to be stationed in such a hazardous region began to take place in the public arena. The central question that was discussed was whether or not a member of the royal family ought to serve in such a perilous environment. On the one hand, there were some individuals working for the Ministry of Defense who were of the opinion that sending Harry to the front lines would put him in dangers that were not absolutely necessary, and that he should instead be shielded from these threats. In a statement that was made public in April of 2006, a spokeswoman for the Ministry of Defense (MOD) said that Harry's "overt presence would attract more attention." To put it another way, due to the fact that Harry would be such a prominent target, the presence of Harry would place both himself and the soldiers he led in a more precarious position. In other words, Harry's presence would make the situation more dangerous.

Throughout the entirety of the discussion, both John Reid, who was serving as Secretary of Defense at the time, and Harry himself took an opposing position. The Prince of Wales officially agreed with Reid's assessment of the situation after Reid defended Harry's right as a commissioned officer to serve on the frontline. Reid defended Harry's right to serve on the frontline. "If they had said, 'no, you can't go frontline,'" Harry explained, "then I wouldn't have dragged my poor ass through Sandhurst, and I wouldn't be where I am now." [Case in point:] "If they had said, 'no, you can't go frontline,'" Harry explained, "then I wouldn't have It seemed likely that Harry would be allowed to fight after all, given that even the MOD had declared in its initial statement that Harry should be able to "undertake the widest spectrum of deployments," given that the MOD had declared that Harry should be able to "undertake the widest spectrum of deployments."

As the weeks and months passed, the contentious debate showed no signs of abating. At one point in time, Harry made a threat to leave the army if he was prevented from going to battle with the rest of his unit so that he could remain safe. He did this so that he could stay out of harm's way. In the end, the decision to send Harry to Iraq as a member of the third mechanized division was finalized and announced by the government in February of 2007. In either May or June of 2007, Harry would embark on his journey to the battlefield.

A Last-Minute Reversal

Even as late as the eighth of April in 2007, it appeared almost certain that Harry would be dispatched. General Sir Richard Dannatt, who was serving as the head of the British Army at the time, stated that he was the one who made the decision to let Harry serve as a troop commander in Iraq on his own volition. Then, all of those plans were abruptly scrapped for no apparent reason.

The 16th of May had arrived, and Harry's departure was getting closer and closer with each passing day. In a surprising turn of events, Dannatt disclosed that Harry would not be going to Iraq after all. This news came as a shock to everyone. At this point, a number of different parties had issued death threats against him, and it was determined that, due to the fact that Harry was seen as a high-value target, he and his men would be in a very precarious situation if he traveled to Iraq. This conclusion was reached after it was discovered that a number of different parties had issued death threats against him.

Harry has been very outspoken about how dissatisfied he is with the current circumstances. On the other hand, as we will see in the following paragraph, he had not yet exhausted all of his options.

Secret Deployment To Afghanistan

It presented Harry with a significant obstacle in the form of the fact that his first assignment was available to the general public. His deployment was something that had been talked about on a few different new sites in the time leading up to it, which started with an announcement that was made one whole year in advance. An adversary of the United Kingdom, NATO, or western society could easily take advantage of the situation and start formulating nefarious strategies with very little effort. When Harry did finally make it to the front lines of the war, he did so under cover of darkness in order to avoid drawing unwanted attention to himself.

In June of 2007, Harry took a trip to CFB Sheffield, which is a military base that is situated west of Medicine Hat in the province of Alberta in Canada. It has come to light that he will be taking part in training alongside members of the Canadian Armed Forces and the British Army in order to get himself ready for the opportunity to serve in Afghanistan. After that, for the remainder of that year, no additional information regarding the Prince was disclosed to the public. The story of where Harry had gone up until the beginning of the following year is when it first became known to the general public. The article was initially printed in the German publication Bild, and then it was reprinted in the New Idea newspaper in Australia. At that point, the proverbial cat was out of the bag, and the British Army had no choice but to announce that Harry had already been secretly sent to Afghanistan and that news of his deployment had been locked down by virtue of a news blackout, which BiM and New Idea had stubbornly breached. Additionally, the British Army had no choice but to announce that Harry had already been secretly sent to Afghanistan and that news of his deployment had been locked down by virtue of a news blackout. In addition, the British Army was compelled to make the announcement that Harry had already been covertly dispatched to Afghanistan and that a news blackout had been implemented to prevent any information regarding his deployment from becoming public.

The British Ministry of Defense issued a statement in February 2008 confirming what earlier leaks had already uncovered: Harry had been serving as a Forward Air Controller in the Helmand Province of Afghanistan for the previous ten weeks, beginning in the latter half of the year 2007. A soldier who is stationed on the ground and provides eyes-on intel and guidance for close air support is known as a Forward Air Controller. This is done for a number of reasons, the primary one being to guarantee that the aircraft hits the designated target while simultaneously causing as little collateral damage as is humanly possible.

In the end, Harry was successful in completing the task he had set out to do. While stationed in Helmand Province, which is located in the southern portion of Afghanistan and is the largest of the country's 34 provinces in terms of area, the Prince had assisted British troops that were made up of Nepalese Gurkha soldiers in repelling an attack by the Taliban. The province is the largest of Afghanistan's 34 provinces in terms of area. In addition to that, as a Forward Air Controller, he had been responsible for patrol duty in areas that were known to be hazardous. He had undoubtedly been placed in a hazardous environment, but he emerged from it unharmed and able to carry out his duties in a competent manner despite the challenges they presented.

As soon as people learned the information, there was a discernible change in the tone of the ongoing conversation that was taking place in the public sphere. It was necessary to evacuate Harry from Afghanistan due to the fact that the media was falling over themselves to cover the story of Harry's "war hero" exploits; however, doing so would only place him, his fellow soldiers, and the journalists in grave danger. The decision to evacuate Harry from Afghanistan was made due to the fact that the media was falling over themselves to cover the story of Harry's "war hero" exploits. On the other hand, it was now common knowledge that Harry possessed the skills necessary to carry out the responsibilities of an officer. In addition to this, he would make history by becoming the first member of the royal family to serve in an active conflict zone since his uncle, Prince Andrew. Moreover, he would be the first member of the royal family to serve in an active conflict zone. Andrew had served as a helicopter pilot during the conflict that took place in Argentina in the 1980s over the Falkland Islands. Now, approximately 25 years later, Harry has joined the ranks of British Royal War Heroes, following in the footsteps of his uncle who served in World War I.

In point of fact, Andrew's legacy would come to mean even more to Harry in the years to come, particularly taking into consideration the fact that the Prince's next move would be to become a helicopter pilot like his uncle had done before him. This turned out to be the path that Harry took to get back to the battleground, as we'll see in the next section; instead of doing it on the ground, he did it in an airplane. This was the route that Harry took.

Additional Training And Relationship

Harry's life picked up where it left off after he returned from his tour in Afghanistan, moving at a breakneck pace. The shenanigans that he had been involved in recently were widely reported on in the media. After being promoted, he was given the rank of lieutenant in April of 2008. The promotion took place in the military. After that, in the following month, Harry's aunt Princess Anne presented him with the Afghan Medal, which is also known as the Operational Service Medal for Afghanistan. This award is in recognition of Harry's service in Afghanistan. Queen Elizabeth has no other children besides her daughter Princess Anne. The event was held at the Combermere Barracks, which is a military station that is situated close to Windsor Castle. The castle served as the venue for the event.

Who else was present to witness that very significant event? The name Chelsy Davy.

Throughout the entirety of 2008, the disagreement between Harry and Chelsy was a popular topic of conversation in the media and across a variety of online sources. There were rumors that they had broken up for a while, but that they later reunited and began hanging out regularly together. Chelsy told their mutual friends on Facebook that they had ended their relationship for good in January of 2009, when she posted the news on the social networking site. Despite this, there are rumors that they got back together and didn't formally end their relationship until sometime in early 2010. It was anticipated that this would take place in 2010. Chelsy Davy was never a part of his life after he completed his first tour in Afghanistan and before he eventually went back to the Middle East to fight in active conflict there. This is a fact, irrespective of the sequence of events that took place between them.

The Defense Helicopter Flying School is a training facility that is based in Shropshire, England, and specializes in teaching aircrews how to operate the Bell Griffin HT1 and the Eurocopter Squirrel HT1. When Harry was a student at this establishment in October of 2008, he was taught how to pilot both the Eurocopter Squirrel HT1 and the Bell Griffin HT1. At the time of Harry's graduation from the academy, his older brother, Prince William, who had graduated from the academy previously and was working as a sub-lieutenant in both the Royal Navy and the Royal Air Force, was presiding over the ceremony. William was disheartened when he found out that, because he was higher in the line of succession to the throne than his sibling, Harry, he would not be able to participate in the battles on the front lines like Harry did. Since William was higher in the line of succession, he would be even more protected than his sibling would be.

A ceremony to present Prince Harry with his wings took place at Middle Wallop Army Air Corps Base in May of 2010. The ceremony was attended by the prince. One may hear these wings referred to as a flying brevet on occasion. They were passed down from Prince Charles to his own son, Prince George of Wales. By April 2011, Harry had been promoted to the rank of Captain and had made significant strides in his training, reaching the point where he now possessed his Apache Flying Badge. As a result of these accomplishments, he was awarded the badge. Soon, he would be given clearance to go back to the front line in Afghanistan, but this time it would be as a pilot for an Apache helicopter. This time, he would be leading the charge against the enemy. It was the only thing left for him to do, and he completed it in the United States, more specifically in the states of California and Arizona. The time that he spent in the state of California will be discussed in greater depth in the chapter that comes after this one.

CHAPTER 5

The Dark Years

In June 2011, Harry responded to a question about his romantic life by saying that he was "100 percent single," but he did not provide any additional information. She did attend Prince William and Catherine Middleton's wedding in April of that year, but Chelsy Davy told the press that she and Harry would not get married because they had fundamental incompatibilities in what they wanted out of life. This statement was made after she attended the wedding of Prince William and Catherine Middleton. Despite the fact that Chelsy Davy was there for the wedding, this outcome occurred.

In 2011, Prince Harry was firmly committed to the life of a bachelor while also finishing his training to become an Apache helicopter pilot. During this time, he also completed his training. On the other hand, one shouldn't place an excessive amount of weight on what they perceive to be on the surface. The emotional arc of Harry's life was heading in a negative direction, and the events that were going to take place over the next couple of years were only going to make things more challenging for him.

The Party Life

After moving to California for his training in October 2011, Harry made rapid strides toward the top of his class and maintained his previous level of success in his new environment. The Blue Angels are a team of pilots that are well-known across the United States, among people who are interested in aviation on both the military and civilian levels. The Naval Air Facility, which can be found just outside of El Centro in California, is a first-rate base that manages the training programs for pilots of a wide variety of aircraft. The Blue Angels, a flight demonstration squadron that performs aerobatics and is based at the Naval Air Facility, are included in this category. Because El Centro has a population of less than 50,000 people, the city does not offer a significant number of opportunities for trainees to engage in entertaining activities during their downtime. This is due to the fact that El Centro's population is less than 50,000. Having said that, San Diego is conveniently located nearby, and the city features a rich assortment of activities for people of all interests.

Harry was quickly discovered by journalists from tabloid publications as well as journalists from more serious publications at popular cafés and shops located all over the city of San Diego. Regular articles providing up-to-date information on his whereabouts and the activities he was participating in across the United

States were published in newspapers located all over the country. And what was it exactly that the media chose to concentrate their attention on? His enthusiasm for getting together with people. The amount of news stories started growing exponentially almost immediately.

Because of this, and also because of the speculation in American newspapers like the Washington Post that the Prince would soon become bored of San Diego and turn his attention to an even bigger party town nearby called Las Vegas, Harry was pulled from his training in the United States and was transported back to England, where he completed his Apache certifications at Wattisham Airfield in Suffolk. This was done because Harry was pulled from his training in the United States and because of the speculation in American newspapers like the Washington Post that the Prince would soon become bored of San Diego and This was done because of the widespread belief that the Prince would soon become dissatisfied with San Diego and begin focusing his attention on Las Vegas instead.

Harry never gave up the party lifestyle, and as a direct consequence, he quickly developed behaviors that were detrimental to himself. The so-called Diamond Jubilee, also known as the 60th anniversary of Queen Elizabeth II's accession to the throne, was celebrated by the monarch throughout the month of February in 2012. This event was also known as the "Diamond Jubilee."

Due to the fact that no other queen of England has been able to maintain her position for the full 60 years that have passed since Queen Victoria, the fact that this event has taken place is a significant cause for celebration. During that time period, Harry went through periods of intense anxiety as well as panic attacks. Because he put in so much effort as an officer and pilot, he would eventually become exhausted and experience burnout as a result of his efforts.

After some time had passed, he reflected back on this period of his life and said, "I wasn't drinking Monday through Friday, but I would probably drink a week's worth in one day on a Friday or a Saturday night."

During this time, Harry was doing a good job of concealing the deterioration that was taking place in his situation. He maintained a high level of performance throughout the entirety of his training, and he was now contemplating the prospect of serving as a helicopter pilot in Afghanistan for a second time. In addition to that, he was successful in his search for a new girlfriend. Cressida Bonas, an English actress and model, became his girlfriend in May of 2012 after Princess Eugenie introduced the two of them to one another. Cressida Bonas was introduced to him by Princess Eugenie. On the other hand, it was obvious that Harry was having problems on the inside. And this was just the start of things getting even worse than they already were.

Return To Afghanistan

On September 7, 2012, Harry arrived in Afghanistan for the second time. This trip lasted for a total of seven days. It was anticipated that everything would work out perfectly in the end. After all, Harry had been working toward the achievement of this objective for a considerable amount of time, and it was finally starting to come to fruition. In addition to that, it would offer him a way to divert his attention while also giving him the possibility of reintroducing some order and consistency into his life. But alas, things didn't work out quite the way that we had hoped they would.

More than a hundred men and women with extensive military training served alongside him in the 662 Squadron, 3 Regiment, Army Air-Corps, which he was a part of. This unit was part of the Army Air-Corps. His mission would require him to fly Apache helicopters in the capacity of a gunner in addition to the co-pilot position. Even though he was the one who pulled the trigger on the aircraft, he would later make a comment about the impact that killing rebels had on him, despite the fact that he was the one who killed them. "We fire when we have to, and unfortunately, this occasionally means taking one life in order to save another." In addition to this, he drew comparisons between piloting the helicopters and participating in video games on a PlayStation or Xbox.

However, playing the roles of a pilot and a soldier were not without their share of challenges and difficulties. As soon as Harry arrived in Afghanistan, the Taliban promptly started making preparations to either execute him or kidnap him, depending on which option they decided to take. Zabiullah Mujahid, a spokesman for the Taliban, stated the following in an interview with Reuters: "We are putting everything we have into getting rid of him, which may mean either killing him or capturing him as a result of our efforts. We have instructed our commanders in Helmand to take any and all measures necessary to eliminate him, and they have been informed of this directive." As a direct result of this, Harry discovered almost immediately that he had a sizable target on his back.

Less than a week after Harry's arrival in the country, there was an attempt made on his life. As a result of the threat, he was compelled to move to a location that offered increased levels of safety.

This time around, the British government offered Harry a greater degree of assistance and support while he was engaged in combat on the front line. Even if there were additional precautions that needed to be taken for his safety, there were no plans in place to have him removed from the country at this time. The Secretary of Defense, Philip Hammond, has stated that the Prince of Wales will be exposed to "the same risk as any other Apache pilot."

Harry's tour of duty in Afghanistan, which had lasted for a combined total of twenty weeks, came to an end in January of 2013, at which point he returned home. In the same year, he was promoted to the position of Apache aircraft commander in July of that same year.

Despite this, the fact that he was present during violent conflict and saw people around him die will have an impact on him in the years to come. Thankfully, as we will see in the chapter that comes after this one, Harry was able to discover a way to deal with everything that he had been through that was traumatic. It would begin with him offering assistance to other people, and eventually, he would also make the effort to look for assistance for himself. In the beginning, he would offer assistance to other people.

CHAPTER 6

Helping Others

As soon as Harry returned home from his second tour in Afghanistan, he began to develop an interest in the plight of military veterans, particularly those who had sustained injuries while serving their country in conflicts overseas, both in the United States and in the United Kingdom. This sparked Harry's interest in the plight of military veterans in the United States and in the United Kingdom. The year 2013 was filled with images of a serious-faced veteran having frank discussions with fellow soldiers who were now missing a limb or were scared by combat in some other way. These images replaced those of a partying Harry going out to clubs or restaurants. These photographs were published in newspapers and tabloids located all over the world.

In January of 2014, the Ministry of Defense bestowed upon Harry the honor of being elevated to the rank of staff officer. Harry's responsibilities in this position include the coordination, planning, and support of the other soldiers under his command. It was expected of him that he would lend his assistance in the preparation and carrying out of significant projects and large commemoration events in and around London as part of the responsibilities that were assigned to him. As a result of the fact that Harry would not be participating in any combat during this duty, he would have more time to contemplate ways in which he could assist the injured, which eventually led to his next significant undertaking.

The Invictus Games

In March of 2014, Harry created the Invictus Games, which are an international sporting event designed especially for wounded, injured, and sick servicemen and women who were either veterans or were still actively serving in the armed forces. The Invictus Games are a multi-sport competition that takes place all over the world. When it came time to choose a moniker for these competitions, which would eventually take the form of the Paralympics, Harry gave the matter a great deal of thought. The indefatigable spirit of our wounded warriors is best encapsulated by the Latin word "invictus," which literally translates to "unconquered."

The events that transpired during Harry's two tours of duty in Afghanistan would later serve as the inspiration for an article that he would write for The Sunday Times and which would be based on his personal experiences. He was subjected to experiences and saw things that would leave an indelible mark on him, but he consciously chose not to dwell on things of that nature after making the decision to protect himself from further trauma. Instead, the valor and bravery of his fellow soldiers inspired him, and he felt compelled to aid those who weren't fortunate enough to return from the front line unscathed. Following his participation in the Warrior Games in the United States, which are based on a similar concept, Harry made the decision to make the establishment of the Invictus Games in the United Kingdom his primary objective.

When it was nearly time for the games to be made available to the public, Harry started promoting them by giving interviews to a variety of media outlets such as BBC Radio 2. In response to a question regarding the games that was posed to him during one of these interviews, he stated that "making sure that we pull this off is practically my full-time job at the moment."

The relationship between Harry and Cressida Bonas came to an end in April of 2014; however, the couple has stated to the media that the breakup was "amicable" and lacked the turmoil that accompanied Harry's previous breakup. Cressida Bonas was Harry's third girlfriend after Ginny Weasley and Hermione Granger.

Beginning at the beginning of 2015, Harry took on a role within the British military that was even more focused on providing assistance to wounded service men. He started volunteering for the Personal Recovery Program, which is organized and managed by the Ministry of Defense. He worked together with a number of organizations that help veterans and wounded warriors to improve the organization of any assistance that he could provide to those groups. This assistance included anything from counseling to financial support.

It would appear that Harry was able to gain the much-needed focus that he lacked in his life by concentrating on helping other people in this way. This served as a form of therapy to assist him in working through the problems that he was experiencing in his own life.

Leaving The Military

The news that Harry would be leaving his position in the British Armed Forces by the end of that year was made public in the spring of 2015, when it was announced to the general public. The same announcement stated that while he was pondering his future, he would continue to work with the MOD on a voluntary basis to continue to bring assistance to injured and ailing veterans through government-sponsored recovery programs. This announcement was made on the same day as the first announcement.

Nevertheless, prior to the conclusion of his service in the armed forces, Prince Harry would spend a total of four weeks stationed in an Australian army barracks as a member of the Australian Defense Force. This portion of his military career would take place in Australia. It is fascinating to ponder the possibility that Harry would go to such great lengths to return to Australia in order to conclude a new chapter of his life story in that location. The very first time was when he was finishing up his schooling and getting ready to enlist in the military during his year off, which is commonly referred to as a gap year.

Following their conclusion, the ten years that Harry spent serving his country in the military would be referred to by Harry as the "happiest days of his life." [Case in point:]

As he had promised, he continued to assist military veterans and wounded service members in a variety of different ways. This assistance was provided to veterans of the armed forces. In the fall of 2015, Prince Harry accompanied First Lady Michelle Obama on a tour of several military installations in the United States. At the same time, he continued to organize charitable events in the United Kingdom with the goal of assisting service members.

Getting Help

In the same month the following year, Prince Harry started dating the stunning American actress Meghan Markle. Their relationship began the previous year. In November of that same year, they made their very first official appearance in public together. She would end up being of tremendous assistance to Harry in working through the issues that he'd carried with him for the better part of his life. Harry had carried these issues with him for the majority of his life.

After participating in the creation of the "Heads Together" mental health awareness campaign together, Harry and Catherine didn't wait long to start dating one another. While they were married, Harry's brother and Catherine, who was now his sister-in-law, worked together at the company. It was necessary for Harry to ensure that his brother, who had encountered all of the same challenges while growing up, received the assistance he required in order for Harry to eventually be convinced to seek the assistance he required for himself. Harry's brother had experienced all of the same difficulties as he did while growing up. In exchange, his brother offered Harry the assistance that he required at the appropriate times.

After a period of time had passed, Harry eventually revealed to his friends that he had begun going to therapy sessions. He thanked his brother for making it possible for him to finally proceed with the move, and he thanked his brother again. According to Harry, "the timing has to be absolutely perfect." "In addition, on a more personal note, my brother served as an incredible source of inspiration and motivation for me. May God rest his soul. He continued to insist that this is not right, that this is not normal, that you need to talk to [someone] about this, and that it's OK for you to talk to someone about it."

Boxing was another activity that he turned to in order to assist him in coping with his nervousness, and he did this because he enjoyed the sport. After all of these years, he was finally ready to talk about the passing of his mother, the struggles he endured as a child, and even more recent tragic occurrences that he had experienced while serving on the front line. He was ready to talk about all of these things because he had finally found the courage to do so.

Following his successful efforts to let the past remain in the past and move on with his life, Harry was ready to proceed to the next stage of his journey. In addition, the young lady who was already by his side was going to play an important part in the direction that he desired his life to go. Harry should get married and start a family now that the time is right.

CHAPTER 7

A Family Man

California is where Meghan spent her childhood, and it was there that both of her parents earned Emmy Awards for their work in the television industries as writers, directors, and directors of photography. Meghan's parents divorced when she was very young, and she spent a lot of time with her father, who worked in the television industry in Hollywood. As a result, she became accustomed to the environment in Hollywood very quickly.

Meghan's interest in acting developed later in life, and she eventually made the decision to pursue a career in both theater and television. However, she had difficulty breaking into the industry for the simple reason that, according to Meghan, her mixed-race heritage made it difficult for her to fit certain roles. This was one of the reasons why she found it difficult to break into the industry. During an interview with CNN, she once said that she didn't feel like she was "black enough for the black roles and I didn't feel like I was white enough for the ones." She eventually got work on a few series, but her big break was without a doubt landing the role of Rachel Zane on the USA series Suits, a role she had on the show from the summer of 2011 until the late 2017 season of the show. She played the role of Rachel Zane from the beginning of the show until the end of the 2017 season. She began playing Rachel Zane on Suits in the summer of 2011, and she remained in the role through the end of the show's run in 2017. When her time on Suits came to an end, she was making a total of $50,000 for each episode she had appeared in during her career as an actress.

Before they divorced, Meghan's husband was a film producer by the name of Trevor Engelson. Their marriage lasted only a short time. They had been dating for a number of years prior to getting married, but they were only married for a little bit more than a year before they got a divorce. The following year, 2016, saw the beginning of Meghan's and Prince Harry's romantic relationship. Because of that occurrence, everything in her life was turned completely upside down.

In both the mainstream media and among the general public, there were a lot of people who approved of Meghan and Harry's relationship, but there were also a lot of trolls and people who disapproved of it. In November of 2016, Harry's communications secretary issued a statement in which the Prince's personal concern was expressed regarding various negative and false statements made about Meghan on the internet and in the media. The statement was issued by Harry's communications secretary. The statements were made by a number of different sources, some of which were published in the media and others on the internet.

They continued to move forward in their relationship in spite of the unfavorable comments that were made about it, and the following year, they started making public appearances together.

Wedding Bells

Prince Charles made the announcement of Prince Harry and Meghan Markle's engagement in November 2017, and the news was met with mostly positive commentary from the media at the time. A great number of individuals have voiced their excitement regarding the possibility of a person of mixed race joining the royal family.

The wedding itself was a highly anticipated event, which is the case with a good number of other royal weddings as well. The fact that Markle was an American celebrity on a popular television show contributed to the status of the wedding as an event of even greater significance. In addition to inviting members of the royal family, they also invited a number of their closest personal friends, a number of the celebrities they admired the most, and a few officials from the local government.

In the meantime, Harry was keeping himself busy by engaging in a variety of activities. He was given the title of Captain General of the Royal Marines at the end of December 2017, which is the title of the ceremonial head of the Royal Marines. He was promoted to this position at the end of December 2017. Prince Philip, Harry's grandfather, had been serving in that capacity prior to Harry's appointment to the position.

On May 19, 2018, for their special occasion, the wedding was held at Windsor Castle, as was stated in the preface of this book. On the same day, his grandmother, Queen Elizabeth II, bestowed upon Prince Harry a number of illustrious titles, including that of Duke of Essex, as a mark of her respect and admiration for him. As a result of his promotions, he was given the titles of Lieutenant Commander in the Royal Navy, Major in the British Army, and Squadron Leader in the Royal Air Force. All three of these titles are in the British Armed Forces.

Following the wedding service, there was a reception for approximately two hundred of the couple's relatives and closest friends who were able to attend.

Married Life

Following their wedding, it seemed as though Harry and Meghan had easily adjusted to life as a married couple. In the beginning, they established their residence in

London at Nottingham Cottage, a quaint house that is situated on the grounds of Kensington Palace. This was where they remained for some time. Over the course of its history, it has frequently been used as a short-term residence by a number of members of the royal family, in addition to employees, employees, and friends of the family.

As soon as it was possible, the pregnancy of Meghan's was confirmed, which encouraged Harry and Meghan to begin looking for larger, more suitable living accommodations in the countryside. The pregnancy of Meghan's was confirmed as soon as it was possible. They moved into Frogmore Cottage, which is located right beside Windsor Castle in close proximity to the royal residence. The renovation of the cottage set the owners back several million pounds' worth of money.

On May 6, 2019, Harry and Meghan welcomed their first child together, a son named Archie Mountbatten-Windsor. This event had been eagerly anticipated for quite some time. Harry's most recent life milestones included becoming a father and a husband. But the happiness of family life wouldn't last forever, and the new family would quickly feel unsettled in their brand-new home in the United Kingdom.

CONCLUSION

The struggles that Harry and Meghan were having within the royal family were mostly unknown to the general world. On the other hand, it became immediately obvious to everyone involved that they would not be remaining in the UK. Following the closure of their office at Buckingham Palace in March of 2020, Prince Harry and Meghan Markle have announced that they will "no longer undertake formal engagements in support of the Queen." Buckingham Palace was the location of their royal office. They left not too long after that to travel throughout the United States and Canada for a period of time. When the couple finally decided to buy a home in Southern California in June, their "short vacation" became a move that would last them a lifetime. Their new home is on the property that formerly belonged to Riven Rock, which is located in Montecito, California. During this time, Harry had also tendered his resignation from every official military position to which he had been appointed prior to this point.

In July, Meghan discovered that she was pregnant, but she ultimately decided to have the pregnancy terminated. During this time, they were effectively cut off from the royal family, and as a result, they renounced any and all responsibilities and ties that they were able to maintain with the family.

During an interview with Oprah Winfrey that took place in 2021, Prince Harry and Meghan Markle discussed their views regarding living in the United Kingdom with the royal family. They admitted, for the first time, that doing so was not something that made them feel comfortable.

These words, of course, caused a great deal of controversy, but Harry and Meghan have both stated publicly that they are simply happier in the United States, where they have created a joyful family life for themselves and where they have grown their careers as actors. Since then, the words have caused a great deal of controversy. On their property, there is even a chicken coop in which they take care of birds who have been rescued from a factory farm.

The year 2021 also witnessed the occurrence of two other significant events. First, Prince Harry and his wife Meghan welcomed their second child, a daughter named Lilibet Mountbatten-Windsor, and Harry created a documentary titled The Me You Can't See, which is about his life and the experiences he has had. The challenging years that followed are discussed in this book, and in the documentary, Harry reveals his thoughts on those years for the very first time.

In 2022, Harry and Meghan made the arduous journey all the way back to the United Kingdom for a solemn occasion: the burial of Harry's grandmother, Elizabeth. It was abundantly clear that despite the fact that they might have had personal issues with the queen and other members of the royal family, they still loved them very much because of how respectful they were and how moved to tears they were during the service of their loved one's funeral.

The story of Harry demonstrates the significance of cultivating a sense of duty and responsibility in its readers. He felt an obligation to his people when he was a young prince, and he felt the same obligation later in life when he was serving his country as a soldier. It wasn't always easy for him to persevere through emotionally trying times, but he did so because he felt a responsibility to his fellow soldiers to do what he could to assist others. He did whatever he could to help others.

Even his profound sense of obligation was not enough to keep him from abdicating his position in the royal family in the end. In what particular way exactly? Because he was now a husband, it was his duty to protect his own family and to do everything in his power to ensure that his wife and children were happy and safe.

Emotionally speaking, Harry went through the wringer, but he came out on the other side of it a stronger father, leader, and person in general. And what he chooses to do with those characteristics today will unquestionably inspire other people to pursue the paths that are unique to them and to lend a hand to those who are located in their immediate surroundings. What possibly could be a better inheritance for someone to leave behind?

The End.

QUESTION AND ANSWER SECTION

Q: If Prince Harry were to start a band, what would they be called?

A: "The Wild Ginger"

Q: What is Prince Harry's favorite comfort food?

A: Prince Harry's favorite comfort food is said to be his Grandmother Queen Elizabeth's recipe for roast chicken.

Q: If Prince Harry could have any superpower, what would it be?

A: If Prince Harry could have any superpower, he would likely choose the ability to teleport to different locations, in order to easily visit the various charitable organizations and causes he supports around the world.

Q: What is Prince Harry's hidden talent?

A: Prince Harry's hidden talent is reportedly his ability to play the guitar. He is said to be quite good and has even performed in public a few times.

Q: If Prince Harry were stranded on a deserted island and could only bring three items, what would they be?

A: If Prince Harry were stranded on a deserted island, he would likely bring a satellite phone to call for help, a water filtration system, and a good book.

Q: What is Prince Harry's favorite pastime?

A: Prince Harry's favorite pastime is said to be playing sports, particularly polo and rugby. He is also known to enjoy hiking, traveling and spending time with his family and friends.

Q: If Prince Harry could have dinner with any historical figure, who would it be?

A: If Prince Harry could have dinner with any historical figure, he might choose his mother, Princess Diana, who was known for her humanitarian work and dedication to charitable causes.

Q: What is Prince Harry's favorite book?

A: Prince Harry's favorite book is unknown, but he has been known to enjoy reading books on history, particularly military history.

Q: What is Prince Harry's favorite quote?

A: Prince Harry's favorite quote is not known, but he has been known to quote his mother Princess Diana, who said, "Carry out a random act of kindness, with no expectation of reward, safe in the knowledge that one day someone might do the same for you."

Q: If Prince Harry could have any pet, what would it be?

A: If Prince Harry could have any pet, he might choose a dog, as he has been known to be a dog lover and has even rescued a few in the past.

Q: If Prince Harry were to create his own holiday, what would it be called and what would it celebrate?

A: If Prince Harry were to create his own holiday, he might call it "Community Day" and it would be a day dedicated to celebrating and encouraging acts of kindness and volunteerism within local communities.

Q: If Prince Harry were to star in a movie, what genre would it be and what character would he play?

A: If Prince Harry were to star in a movie, he might choose to play a historical figure such as King Henry V, known for his bravery and leadership in the Battle of

Agincourt. He would probably fit in a war and historical genre.

Q: If Prince Harry were to write a book, what would it be about?

A: If Prince Harry were to write a book, it might be about his experiences as a member of the royal family, and the work he's done with various charitable organizations and causes he's passionate about. He might also include a reflection on his mother Princess Diana's humanitarian legacy and how it has shaped his own perspective and actions

Q: If Prince Harry were to host a talk show, what would the topic be and who would be his first guest?

A: If Prince Harry were to host a talk show, it would likely be focused on mental health and well-being, and his first guest might be someone who has overcome personal struggles in this area and can share their inspiring story.

Q: If Prince Harry were to open a business, what would it be?

A: If Prince Harry were to open a business, he might open a sustainable eco-tourism company that focuses on preserving and promoting natural environments while providing unique and meaningful experiences for travelers.

Q: What was Princess Diana's favourite charitable cause?

A: Princess Diana's favourite charitable cause was helping people affected by HIV/AIDS. She was known for her tireless efforts to raise awareness and combat the stigma surrounding the disease.

Q: What was Princess Diana's favourite hobby?

A: Princess Diana's favourite hobby was dancing. She was known to be a gifted dancer and enjoyed both ballroom and modern dance.

Q: What was Princess Diana's favourite flower?

A: Princess Diana's favourite flower was the white rose.

Q: What was Princess Diana's favourite fashion statement?

A: Princess Diana's favorite fashion statement was her iconic "little black dress", which she was often seen wearing in public.

Q: What was Princess Diana's favourite song?

A: Princess Diana's favourite song was "Candle in the Wind" by Elton John.

Q: How did Prince Harry meet Meghan Markle?

A: Prince Harry met Meghan Markle through a mutual friend in July 2016.

Q: What was the theme of Prince Harry and Meghan Markle's wedding?

A: The theme of Prince Harry and Meghan Markle's wedding was "the celebration of love."

Q: Where did Prince Harry and Meghan Markle's honeymoon take place?

A: Prince Harry and Meghan Markle's honeymoon destination is not publicly known, but it was reported that they went on a private safari in Africa.

Q: How long have Prince Harry and Meghan Markle been married?

A: Prince Harry and Meghan Markle have been married since May 19, 2018.

Q: What is the name of Prince Harry and Meghan Markle's first child?

A: Prince Harry and Meghan Markle's first child is named Archie Harrison Mountbatten-Windsor.

Q: Why did Prince Harry leave the military?

A: Prince Harry left the military in June 2015, after completing two tours of duty in Afghanistan and several other deployments. He decided to leave the military in order to focus on his charitable work and pursue other personal projects.

Q: What was Prince Harry's rank in the military?

A: Prince Harry's rank in the military was Captain.

Q: What were Prince Harry's roles and responsibilities in the military?

A: Prince Harry served in the British Army for 10 years. During that time, he served as an Apache helicopter pilot, and also worked in various staff roles such as training, public relations and administration.

Q: How long did Prince Harry serve in the military?

A: Prince Harry served in the military for 10 years, from 2005 to 2015.

Q: What was Prince Harry's most notable achievement in the military?

A: Prince Harry's most notable achievement in the military was his two tours of duty in Afghanistan as an Apache helicopter pilot. He flew over 20 missions, providing close air support to troops on the ground, and was decorated with medals for his service.

Q: How did Princess Diana die?

A: Princess Diana died in a car crash on August 31, 1997. The crash occurred in the Pont de l'Alma tunnel in Paris, France while she was being pursued by paparazzi.

Q: Who was with Princess Diana when she died?

A: Princess Diana was with her companion, Dodi Fayed, and their driver, Henri Paul, when the crash occurred. Both Dodi Fayed and Henri Paul also died in the crash.

Q: How old was Princess Diana when she died?

A: Princess Diana was 36 years old when she died.

Q: What was the public reaction to Princess Diana's death?

A: The public reaction to Princess Diana's death was one of shock and grief. People around the world were deeply saddened by the loss of the "People's Princess" and thousands of mourners gathered outside Kensington Palace and Buckingham Palace to pay their respects.

Q: What were the circumstances surrounding Princess Diana's death?

A: The exact circumstances surrounding Princess Diana's death are still debated. The official investigation concluded that the crash was caused by the driver's high speed and alcohol consumption. However, there have been some conspiracy theories that suggest that the crash was planned.

A STUDY GUIDE ON PRINCE HARRY BIOGRAPHY

Introduction:

Prince Harry, also known as Prince Henry Charles Albert David of Wales, was born on September 15, 1984. He is the younger son of Prince Charles and Princess Diana and the younger brother of Prince William. Prince Harry is known for his charitable work, military service, and his role as a member of the British royal family.

Early Life:

Prince Harry was born in London, England. He is the second son of Prince Charles and Princess Diana and the younger brother of Prince William. He was raised in Kensington Palace and attended schools such as Wetherby School, Ludgrove School, and Eton College.

Military Service:

Prince Harry served in the British Army for 10 years, from 2005 to 2015. He served as an Apache helicopter pilot, and also worked in various staff roles such as training, public relations and administration. He completed two tours of duty in Afghanistan and several other deployments. He decided to leave the military in order to focus on his charitable work and pursue other personal projects.

Charitable Work:

Prince Harry is known for his charitable work and dedication to various causes such as mental health, veterans' issues, and conservation. He has been involved with a number of organizations, including the Invictus Games, which supports wounded and sick servicemen and women through sports. He also established the Sentebale charity, which helps children affected by HIV/AIDS in Lesotho, southern Africa.

Marriage and Family:

Prince Harry married Meghan Markle, an American actress, on May 19, 2018. They have one child, Archie Harrison Mountbatten-Windsor.

Death of Princess Diana:

Princess Diana, Prince Harry's mother died in a car crash on August 31, 1997. The crash occurred in the Pont de l'Alma tunnel in Paris, France while she was being pursued by paparazzi. The public reaction to Princess Diana's death was one of shock and grief. The exact circumstances surrounding Princess Diana's death are still debated.

Key Points to Remember:

Prince Harry is the younger son of Prince Charles and Princess Diana and the younger brother of Prince William.

He served in the British Army for 10 years and completed two tours of duty in Afghanistan.

He is known for his charitable work and dedication to various causes such as mental health, veterans' issues, and conservation.

He married Meghan Markle in 2018 and they have one child.

His mother, Princess Diana died in a car crash in 1997.

Further Reading:

"Harry: Life, Loss, and Love" by Katie Nicholl

"Prince Harry: The Inside Story" by Penny Junor

"Diana: Her True Story" by Andrew Morton

Quiz:

- What is Prince Harry's real name?
- What is Prince Harry's occupation before he left the military?
- What is the name of Prince Harry and Meghan Markle's first child?
- What was the theme of Prince Harry and Meghan Markle's wedding?
- What is the name of the charity established by Prince Harry to help children affected by HIV/AIDS in Lesotho?
- How did Princess Diana die?
- What is Prince Harry's favorite hobby?
- What was the public reaction to Princess Diana's death?
- What are the causes that Prince Harry is known for dedicating himself to?
- What is the name of the organization that supports wounded and sick servicemen and women through sports, established by Prince Harry?

STUDY GUIDE ABOUT PRINCE HARRY BOOK "SPARE"

Introduction:

"Spare" is an autobiography written by Prince Harry, also known as Prince Henry Charles Albert David of Wales. In this book, Prince Harry reflects on his life and experiences, including his time in the military, his charitable work, and his relationship with his family. The book is an intimate look into the life of a member of the British royal family and offers insight into the personal struggles and triumphs of Prince Harry.

Background and Overview:

In "Spare," Prince Harry opens up about his experience growing up in the royal family, dealing with the media attention and the loss of his mother, Princess Diana. He also writes about his time in the military, including his deployment to Afghanistan and the impact that it had on him. He also talks about the causes and organizations that he's been involved with, such as the Invictus Games, and the Sentebale charity. He also writes about his relationship with Meghan Markle, and how they started to build a new life together, and the challenges that they faced.

Key Points to Remember:

"Spare" is an autobiography written by Prince Harry.

In the book, Prince Harry reflects on his life and experiences, including his time in the military, his charitable work, and his relationship with his family.

He writes about his experience growing up in the royal family and the impact of the media attention and the loss of his mother, Princess Diana.

He also talks about his time in the military, including his deployment to Afghanistan and the impact that it had on him.

He also writes about his relationship with Meghan Markle and how they started to build a new life together, and the challenges that they faced.

Themes:

Family: Prince Harry writes about his relationship with his family, particularly his mother, Princess Diana and his father, Prince Charles. He also writes about the impact of losing his mother at a young age, and how it has shaped him throughout his life.

Military Service: Prince Harry writes about his experience serving in the military, including his deployment to Afghanistan, and how it has affected him both emotionally and physically.

Charitable Work: Prince Harry writes about the causes and organizations that he's been involved with, such as the Invictus Games and Sentebale charity, and how they've given him purpose in life.

Relationship: Prince Harry writes about his relationship with Meghan Markle and how they started to build a new life together, and the challenges that they faced.

Further Reading:

"Harry: Life, Loss, and Love" by Katie Nicholl

"Prince Harry: The Inside Story" by Penny Junor

"Diana: Her True Story" by Andrew Morton

Quiz:

- What is the name of the autobiography written by Prince Harry?
- What are the main themes in the book?
- What did Prince Harry write about his experience growing up in the royal family?
- What did Prince Harry write about his time in the military?
- What did Prince Harry write about his relationship with Meghan Markle?

- What are the name of the causes and organizations that Prince Harry has been involved with?
- What did Prince Harry write about his experience losing his mother, Princess Diana?
- What are the challenges that Prince Harry and Meghan Markle faced in their new life together?
- What is the impact of Prince Harry's deployment to Afghanistan?
- How does Prince Harry's charitable work give him purpose in life?

Thanks For Reading.

Printed in Great Britain
by Amazon